People in My Community/La gente de mi comunidad

Nurse/
El enfermero

Carol Stream Public Library
Carol Stream, Illinois 60188

JoAnn Early Macken
photographs by/fotografías de Gregg Andersen

Reading consultant/Consultora de lectura: Susan Nations, M.Ed., author/literacy coach/consultant

WEEKLY WR READER®
EARLY LEARNING LIBRARY

Please visit our web site at: **www.earlyliteracy.cc**
**For a free color catalog describing Weekly Reader® Early Learning Library's
list of high-quality books, call 1-877-445-5824 (USA) or 1-800-387-3178 (Canada).
Weekly Reader® Early Learning Library's fax: (414) 336-0164.**

Library of Congress Cataloging-in-Publication Data available upon request
from publisher. Fax (414) 336-0157 for the attention of the Publishing
Records Department.

ISBN 0-8368-3673-1 (lib. bdg.)
ISBN 0-8368-3687-1 (softcover)

First published in 2003 by
Weekly Reader® Early Learning Library
330 West Olive Street, Suite 100
Milwaukee, WI 53212 USA

Copyright © 2003 by Weekly Reader® Early Learning Library

Art direction: Tammy Gruenewald
Page layout: Katherine A. Goedheer
Photographer: Gregg Andersen
Editorial assistant: Diane Laska-Swanke
Translators: Colleen Coffey and Consuelo Carrillo

Printed in the United States of America

1 2 3 4 5 6 7 8 9 07 06 05 04 03

Note to Educators and Parents

Reading is such an exciting adventure for young children! They are beginning to integrate their oral language skills with written language. To encourage children along the path to early literacy, books must be colorful, engaging, and interesting; they should invite the young reader to explore both the print and the pictures.

People in My Community is a new series designed to help children read about the world around them. In each book young readers will learn interesting facts about some familiar community helpers.

Each book is specially designed to support the young reader in the reading process. The familiar topics are appealing to young children and invite them to read — and re-read — again and again. The full-color photographs and enhanced text further support the student during the reading process.

In addition to serving as wonderful picture books in schools, libraries, homes, and other places where children learn to love reading, these books are specifically intended to be read within an instructional guided reading group. This small group setting allows beginning readers to work with a fluent adult model as they make meaning from the text. After children develop fluency with the text and content, the book can be read independently. Children and adults alike will find these books supportive, engaging, and fun!

Una nota a los educadores y a los padres

¡La lectura es una emocionante aventura para los niños! En esta etapa están comenzando a integrar su manejo del lenguaje oral con el lenguaje escrito. Para fomentar la lectura desde una temprana edad, los libros deben ser vistosos, atractivos e interesantes; deben invitar al joven lector a explorar tanto el texto como las ilustraciones.

La gente de mi comunidad es una nueva serie pensada para ayudar a los niños a conocer el mundo que los rodea. En cada libro, los jóvenes lectores conocerán datos interesantes sobre el trabajo de distintas personas de la comunidad.

Cada libro ha sido especialmente diseñado para facilitar el proceso de lectura. La familiaridad con los temas tratados atrae la atención de los niños y los invita a leer — y releer — una y otra vez. Las fotografías a todo color y el tipo de letra facilitan aún más al estudiante el proceso de lectura.

Además de servir como fantásticos libros ilustrados en la escuela, la biblioteca, el hogar y otros lugares donde los niños aprenden a amar la lectura, estos libros han sido concebidos específicamente para ser leídos en grupos de instrucción guiada. Este contexto de grupos pequeños permite que los niños que se inician en la lectura trabajen con un adulto cuya fluidez les sirve de modelo para comprender el texto. Una vez que se han familiarizado con el texto y el contenido, los niños pueden leer los libros por su cuenta. ¡Tanto niños como adultos encontrarán que estos libros son útiles, entretenidos y divertidos!

— Susan Nations, M.Ed., author, literacy coach,
and consultant in literacy development

A nurse works hard to help people feel healthy. Nurses help take care of people who are injured or sick.

- - - - - - - -

La enfermera trabaja duro para ayudar a la gente a sentirse bien de salud. Los enfermeros cuidan de las personas heridas o enfermas.

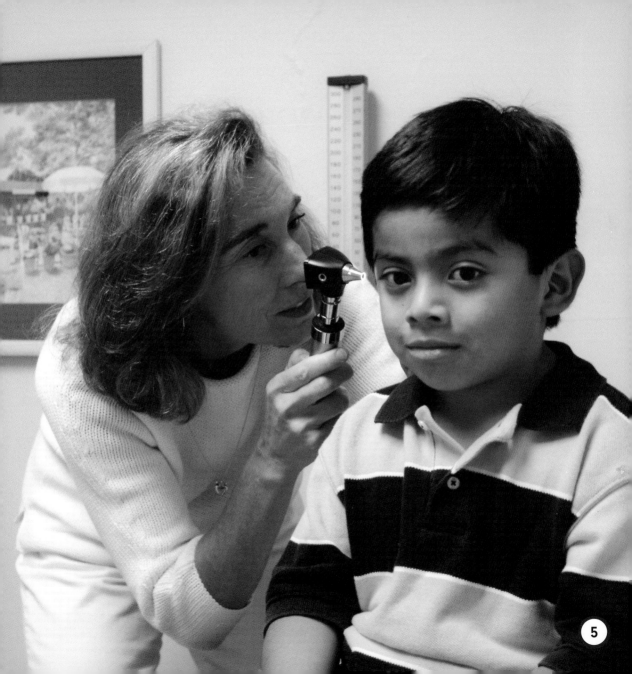

Some nurses work in doctors' offices or hospitals. Some nurses work in schools or factories. Some visit people at home.

- - - - - - - -

Algunos enfermeros trabajan en consultorios médicos o en clínicas. Otros trabajan en las escuelas o las fábricas. A veces visitan los hogares de sus pacientes.

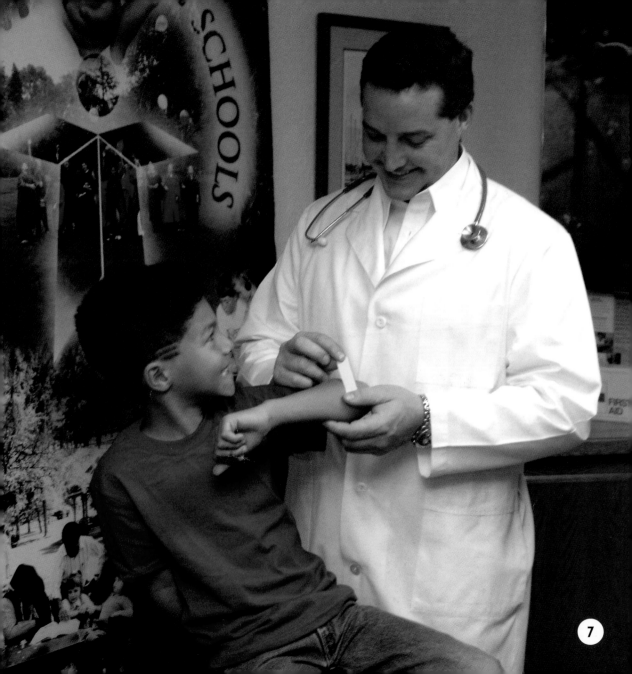

Some nurses wear white **uniforms** and shoes. Some wear colored uniforms or loose shirts and pants.

— — — — — — —

Algunos enfermeros llevan uniformes y zapatos blancos. Otros usan **uniformes** de colores diferentes o camisas y pantalones sueltos.

uniform/uniforme

9

A nurse uses a thermometer to check a patient's temperature. A nurse uses a **stethoscope** to listen to a patient's heartbeat.

— — — — — — — —

La enfermera usa un termómetro para tomar la temperatura del paciente. Ella usa el **estetoscopio** para escuchar los latidos del corazón del paciente.

stethoscope/
estetoscopio

A nurse uses a watch to check a patient's pulse and a **cuff** and a stethoscope to measure blood pressure.

La enfermera usa un reloj para tomar el pulso del paciente. El **tensiómetro** y el estetoscopio ayudan a la enfermera a medir la presión del sangre.

cuff/tensiómetro

13

A nurse weighs patients on a **scale**. Do you know how much you weigh?

– – – – – – – –

La enfermera pesa a los pacientes en una **balanza**. ¿Sabes cuánto pesas?

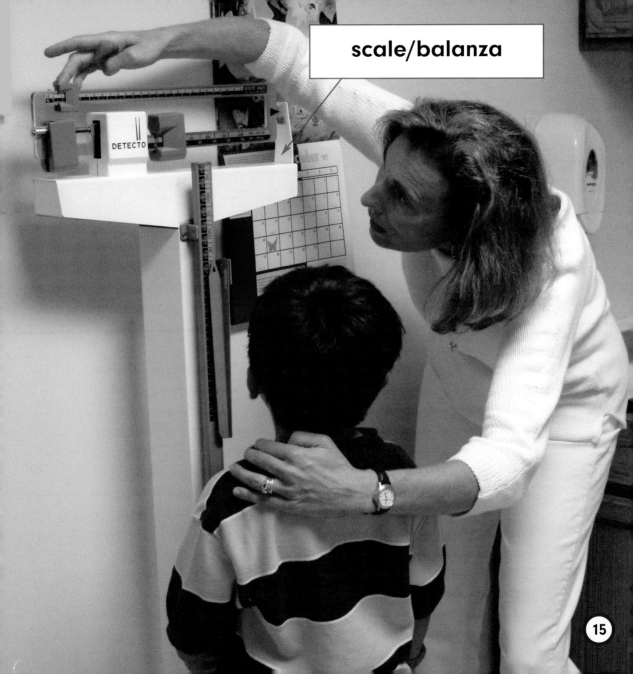

scale/balanza

15

Nurses ask patients questions about their health. They write all the information in each patient's **chart**.

‒ ‒ ‒ ‒ ‒ ‒ ‒

Los enfermeros hacen preguntas a los pacientes sobre su salud. Escriben toda la información de cada paciente en su **historia clínica**.

chart/historia clínica

Nurses do more than give patients medicine. They also teach people how to take care of themselves and their families.

Los enfermeros además de dar medicina a los pacientes, les enseñan cómo cuidarse ellos mismos y cuidar a sus familias.

Nurses take good care of people. If you are ever injured or sick, you can count on a nurse to help you.

- - - - - - - -

Los enfermeros cuidan bien a la gente. Si estás enfermo o herido algún día, puedes contar con una enfermera para ayudarte.

Glossary/Glosario

blood pressure — the amount of force pushing on the blood vessels

presión de la sangre — cantidad de fuerza que reciben los vasos sanguíneos

pulse — the number of heartbeats in a time period

pulso — número de latidos del corazón en un período de tiempo

temperature — the degree of heat in a body

temperatura — grado de calor del cuerpo

uniform — clothing worn by members of a group such as mail carriers, firefighters, or nurses

uniforme — ropa que llevan los miembros de un grupo tales como carteros, bomberos o enfermeros

For More Information/Más información

Fiction Books/Libros de ficción

Lakin, Patricia. *The Mystery Illness.*
  Austin, Texas: Raintree Steck-Vaughn, 1995.

Nonfiction Books/Libros de no ficción

Liebman, Daniel. *I Want to Be a Nurse.*
  Willowdale, Ont.: Firefly Books, 2001.
Ready, Dee. *Nurses.* Mankato, Minn.:
  Bridgestone Books, 1997.
Schaefer, Lola M. *We Need Nurses.* Mankato, Minn.:
  Pebble Books, 2000.

Web Sites/Páginas Web

Going to the Hospital
www.kidshealth.org/kid/feel_better/places/hospital.html
What happens if you go to the hospital

Index/Índice

About the Author/Información sobre la autora

JoAnn Early Macken is the author of children's poetry, two rhyming picture books, *Cats on Judy* and *Sing-Along Song* and various other nonfiction series. She teaches children to write poetry and received the Barbara Juster Esbensen 2000 Poetry Teaching Award. JoAnn is a graduate of the MFA in Writing for Children Program at Vermont College. She lives in Wisconsin with her husband and their two sons.

JoAnn Early Macken es autora de poesía para niños. Ha escrito dos libros de rimas con ilustraciones, *Cats on Judy* y *Sing-Along Song* y otras series de libros educativos para niños. Ella enseña a los niños a escribir poesía y ha ganado el Premio Barbara Juster Esbensen en el año 2000. JoAnn se graduó con el título de "MFA" en el programa de escritura infantil de Vermont College. Vive en Wisconsin con su esposo y sus dos hijos.